DIE KUNSTHOF PASSAGE DRESDEN

アート横丁

THELEM 2001

INHALT
Contents

20 HOF DER FABELWESEN
Courtyard of the Fabulous Creatures

32 HOF DES LICHTS
Courtyard of Light

40 HOF DER METAMORPHOSEN
Courtyard of the Metamorphoses

50 HOF DER ELEMENTE
Courtyard of the Elements

INTRO » » » » » » » » » » » » » »

Als Kind sei es ihm so vorgekommen, erinnert sich Peter Härtling, »als feierten Dresdens Bewohner zwischen den prächtigen Häusern … ein nie enden wollendes Fest.« Auch wenn von der Barockarchitektur nur Erinnerungsstücke geblieben sind, spukt der *genius loci* lebendiger denn je in den Hügeln am Fluß, den Gärten der Vorstädte und den Bars, Kneipen und Hinterhöfen der Neustadt. Und an wenigen Plätzen wurde er zuletzt so oft angetroffen wie in der Kunsthofpassage.

German poet Peter Härtling recalls visiting Dresden when he was a child: »It always seemed to me that the people there celebrated a never-ending party in their beautiful houses.« Today, only few Baroque-style houses are still standing. Nevertheless, the genius loci is more alive than ever. It roams the hills overlooking the river, the suburban gardens, parks, cafes, bars, and squares, and haunts the courtyards of the Neustadt. Nowhere is it more alive than in the Kunsthof Passage.

Ganz genau kann niemand mehr sagen, was zuerst da war: Die städtebauliche Herausforderung, heruntergekommene Hinterhöfe zu revitalisieren? Die merkantile Frage, wie man im Osten Deutschlands Hinterhäuser vermietet? Die soziale Idee, Wohnen, Arbeiten und Feiern zusammenzubringen? Die pure Lust am Gestalten? Die halb sentimentale, halb ironische Erinnerung an heiße Nächte in Madrid? – Das Ergebnis, die Dresdner Kunsthofpassage, hat jedenfalls von jedem etwas. Und angefangen hat ihre Geschichte irgendwann 1997, als das denkmalgeschützte Haus Alaunstraße 70 saniert wurde und sich fast zwangsläufig die Frage stellte, was mit dem dazugehörigen Hinterhof geschehen sollte. Die alte Nutzung (Brennstoffhandel) war nicht mehr zeitgemäß, die angeblich zeitgemäße (Park- und Abstellplatz) fand der Projektentwickler Tankred Lenz asozial und banausisch. Also mußte etwas Besonde-

Today, nobody can say for certain what the initial stimulus was: The need to revitalize a row of seedy backyards in the interest of urban development; the economic question of how to rent houses in these backyards profitably; the social idea of uniting the concepts of living, working, and celebrating; the simple desire to create something; or a half-ironic, half-sentimental reminiscence of some hot nights in Madrid. Ultimately, it does not matter. The end result, the Kunsthof Passage, contains a bit of it all. Its story began sometime in 1997, when the house at Alaunstraße 70, which has been given monument status, was about to be reconstructed and the question of what to do with the backyard arose. The former use for the backyard (which was the sale of coal) was now obsolete, and its proposed contemporary use as a parking lot was completely unacceptable to Tankred Lenz, developer of the house. In his search for a more appealing alterna-

res her. Vorbilder fanden sich schließlich schnell: konzeptionell die Hackeschen und anderen Höfe in Berlin-Mitte und die Straßencafés mediterraner Städte, formal die surreal anmutenden Fassaden des katalanischen Architekten Antoni Gaudí, die originellen Wohnhausprojekte Friedensreich Hundertwassers und die urtümlichen Plastiken Niki de Saint Phalles. Mit den Passagen, die im 19. Jahrhundert in Städten wie Paris, Mailand, Moskau oder Leipzig entstanden – »glasgedeckten marmorgetäfelten Gängen durch ganze Häusermassen, deren Besitzer sich zu solchen Spekulationen vereinigt haben« –, hat die Dresdner Kunsthofpassage nur wenig gemein. Noch weniger allerdings mit den seit den 1980er Jahren auch in Europa aus dem Boden schießenden Malls nach nordamerikanischem Vorbild, die – je nachdem, was der zuständige Marketing-Director für verkaufsfördernd hält – meist »Center«, oft aber auch »Galerie« oder eben »Passage« heißen. In den ›klassischen‹ Passagen wird die Straße unters Dach gebracht, um Shopping unabhängig vom Wetter und unbelästigt vom Verkehr zu ermöglichen. Die Kunsthofpassage ist zwar (selbstredend!) auch verkehrsfrei, das Verhältnis von Innen zu Außen aber eher umgekehrt: Die Höfe sind gleichsam geschützte Innenräume im Freien, und das Dach über dem Ganzen ist ideeller Natur.

Und die Kunst? In den prächtigen Ausstattungen der Passagen des 19. Jahrhunderts »tritt die Kunst in

tive, Lenz reflected upon many of the places he had visited for some good examples: from a conceptual standpoint, there were the Hackeschen Höfe and other courtyards of downtown Berlin, as well as the café houses lining the streets of cities in the Mediterranean; and from a formal perspective, the surreal facades designed by Catalan architect Antoni Gaudí, the original housing projects of Austrian artist and architect Friedensreich Hundertwasser, and the archaic-looking figures of Niki de Saint Phalles. The Kunsthof Passage in Dresden has little in common with the passages built in the 19th century in Paris, Milan, Moscow, and Leipzig, whose wide walkways consisted of marble floors and glass roofs and traversed whole city blocks.

The Kunsthof Passage has even less in common with the American-style malls that began to appear in Europe in the 1980s, which, owing to some dark and random decisions, were called »centers,« »galeries,« or simply »passages.« Classical passages typically bring the street under a roof, making it possible for people to shop without concern for the weather or automobile traffic. Of course, there is no car traffic in the Kunsthof Passage either, but the relationship between the inside and outside is just the opposite. Here the yards have been rededicated into safe interiors under the open sky. The »roof« is a conceptual one.

And what about art? In the splendid decor of the 19th century passages, »art

den Dienst des Kaufmanns« (Walter Benjamin), in den modernen Malls ist sie gewöhnlich ganz entbehrlich. In der Kunsthofpassage schließlich soll sie als eigenständiges Element der gestalteten Lebensumwelt anregen zu eigener Kreativität.

Eines haben die Passagen dann doch alle gemeinsam: Immer schon waren sie Tummelplätze für Flaneure, jene begnadeten Selbstdarsteller(innen) des Sehen- und-Gesehen-Werdens, die Detektive und Verdächtige, Käufer und Ware zugleich sind. Und tatsächlich erschließt sich die Kunsthofpassage am schönsten im Zeitmaß des Flanierens. 1829 soll es in Paris sogar Mode gewesen sein, dabei eine Schildkröte an der Leine mitzuführen…

indentured the merchant« (Walter Benjamin), whereas modern malls live well without any art at all. The role of art in the Kunsthof Passage as an independent element of the arranged life environment is to stimulate the creativity of those who view it.

Nevertheless, one commonality exists among all of these various types of passages: They have always been the playgrounds of the flaneurs, the gifted actors of seeing and being seen, who are at once detectives and suspects, consumers and the merchandise they purchase. Indeed, it is best to discover the Kunsthof Passage at the leisurely pace of the flaneur. In 1829, it was considered fashionable to be accompanied by a leashed turtle…

Nächste Doppelseite: Die Läden / *Next Doublepage: The Shops*

AUF DEM SANDE – IN DEN SAND

Eine kurze Geschichte der Äußeren Neustadt bis 1990
A Short History of the Dresden Neustadt until 1990

In Dresden ist die Neustadt die ältere Stadt. Das ist keine Posse, mit der die Dresdner ihre Gäste zu verwirren suchen, sondern eine Laune der wechselvollen Stadtgeschichte. Als »Alten-Dresden« nämlich wurde die heutige Neustadt 1313 erstmals urkundlich erwähnt und gab, obwohl sie lange außerhalb der Befestigungen lag, der Stadt ihren Namen. 1685 brannte »Alten-Dresden« fast vollständig ab. Auf dem Gelände wurde – teilweise nach dem großzügigen ›Stadtentwicklungskonzept‹ des Oberlandbaumeisters Johann Caspar von Klengel (1630-1691) – eine Barockstadt angelegt, die 1732 in »Neue Königstadt« umbenannt wurde. Seither ist »Alten-Dresden« eben die »Neustadt«.

Das heute dicht besiedelte Gebiet zwischen der Königsbrücker Straße im Westen und dem Flüßchen Prießnitz im Osten bot noch Anfang des 19. Jahrhunderts ein eher ländliches Bild. Genaugenommen war es nach jahrhundertelangen Abholzungen sogar eine Art Wüste. »Auf dem Sande«, wie das Areal vor den Stadttoren genannt wurde, befanden sich lediglich einige einzelne Gehöfte und eine Alaunhütte (der die heutige Alaunstraße ihren Namen verdankt). Im Westen wurden die Verurteilten gehenkt und zur Abschreckung oft wochenlang hängen gelassen; im Norden übte die sächsische Artillerie.

Erst nach der teilweisen Zerstörung der »Neuen Königstadt« durch die preußische Armee 1763 begann die Besiedelung der späteren Äußeren Neustadt. Der Hauptteil der heutigen Bebauung indessen stammt aus den sogenannten Gründerjahren zwischen 1870 und 1900. Dennoch ist die Äußere Neustadt keine Mietskasernenstadt wie etwa der Prenzlauer Berg im nahen

The Neustadt, which literally means »New Town,« is the old part of Dresden. This name is not a trick to confuse visitors but instead owes itself to a caprice within the changeable history of the city. The Neustadt was first mentioned in 1313 as »Alten-Dresden« (literally »Old Dresden«) and, despite being situated outside the fortification of the city for a lengthy period of time, this was the name given to the town. In 1685, it burned down completely. Following a large-scale plan directed by the Landbaumeister (Saxon state architect) Johann Caspar von Klengel (1630-1691), a modern (i.e. Baroque-style) city was built over the ruins and, in 1732, was renamed »Neue Königsstadt« (literally »New King's Town«). Since then, Alten-Dresden has been known as the Neustadt.

Though today densely populated, the area bound by the Königsbrücker Straße to the west and the little river Prießnitz to the east was still very rural at the beginning of the 19th century. After having undergone hundreds of years of deforestation, the area had become a kind of desert and was, therefore, aptly dubbed »Auf dem Sande« (meaning »on the sand«). The only buildings that existed were a few farmhouses and an alum (»alaun«) factory, from which the name »Alaunstraße« was derived. In the western part of the area, convicts were hanged and were sometimes even left hanging for weeks for didactic purposes. The Saxon artillery was stationed in the north.

Not until the Neue Königsstadt was partially destroyed by Prussian troops in 1763 did the settlement of the later Äußere Neustadt begin. Furthermore, most of the buildings there date back to the period from 1870 to 1900, otherwise known in Ger-

Das bürgerliche Zeitalter in Deutschland neigt sich seinem unheimlichen Ende zu. Blick von Südosten in die Alaunstraße um 1934.

Dieses Detail der prachtvollen Deckenbemalung im Eingang des zum Kunsthof gehörenden Gebäudes Alaunstraße 70 zeigt die heutige Äußere Neustadt um 1830.

The bourgeois era nears an uncanny end: A view of the Alaunstraße from the southeast in 1934.

Detail of the splendid ceiling painting inside the entrance of the building at Alaunstraße 70 which belongs to the Kunsthof Passage. The painting depicts the Neustadt circa 1830.

13

Berlin. Strenge Auflagen des Sächsischen Gesamtministeriums und die Tatsache, daß hier neben Arbeitern immer auch Beamte und Militärs, Intellektuelle und Künstler lebten, verliehen der geschlossenen Bebauung das Flair bürgerlicher Urbanität.

Die Äußere Neustadt blieb von den Luftangriffen vom Februar 1945 und der »Klar-Schiff-Mentalität« der 1950er und 1960er Jahre weitgehend verschont.
Heute gilt sie als eines der schönsten und größten Gründerzeitviertel Europas. Zwar sollen in den 1980er Jahren Pläne zum großflächigen Abriß und »sozialistischen Neuaufbau« existiert haben, diese scheiterten aber entweder am chronischen Geldmangel der staatlichen Bauwirtschaft oder am sanften Widerstand der Dresdner, der sich mentalitätstypisch vor allem im erfolgreichen Hinhalten und geschmeidigen Ausweichen manifestierte.

Allerdings tat der berühmte Zahn der Zeit – großzügig assistiert vom sozialistischen Schlendrian – das seinige. Anfang der 1990er Jahre war, was »Auf dem Sande« begann, in den Sand gefahren. Der größte Teil der Neustadt befand sich in erbärmlichem Zustand. 92 % der Gebäude hatten mittlere bis schwere Schäden. Der Ausstattungsgrad entsprach dem Standard der ersten Jahrhunderthälfte: 95 % der Wohnungen besaßen Ofenheizungen, 79 % WCs »auf halber Treppe«. Daß man letzteres heute bereits erklären muß, zeigt, wie gründlich in den 1990ern saniert und modernisiert wurde: »auf halber Treppe« bedeutete im Falle eines menschlichen Bedürfnisses: raus aus der Wohnung, eine halbe Treppe hinab in eine meist ungeheizte Kammer usw.

Wiederum Endzeitstimmung. Die Alaunstraße von Nordwesten 1986: jedem Trabbi seinen eigenen Parkplatz.

At the end of time again: The Alaunstraße from the northwest in 1986. A parking slot for each and every »Trabbi.« (The »Trabant« was the most common car of the GDR. Built in nearly the same manner from 1958 until the end of production in 1990, it served as a symbol of the socialist idea of prosperity.)

many as the »Founders' Years« of fast-growing capitalism. Nevertheless, the Neustadt did not become an area of tenement houses for the working class like the famous Prenzlauer Berg in nearby Berlin, as strict regulations prevented this from happening. Moreover, in addition to workers, many public officials, artists and intellectuals also dwelled in the Neustadt. This created an atmosphere of bourgeois urbanity in the area.

The Neustadt was more or less spared the destruction of the February 1945 bombing of Dresden, as well as the mentality of suppression and »tidying up« which characterized the 1950s and '60s in Germany. For these reasons, the Neustadt is one of nicest and largest of all the late 19 th century neighborhoods to have been preserved in Europe. While it is true that plans were made in the 1980s to tear down entire city blocks and replace them with the standardized architecture of the communist GDR, these plans never came to fruition, due to a chronic lack of funding as well as to the tender resistance of the inhabitants, which—in accordance with the typical Dresdener mentality—manifested itself in renitent delaying and flexible dodging.

Nevertheless, time, generously assisted by the socialists' dawdling, did take its toll, so that by 1990 most of the buildings were in a miserable state of disrepair. Ninety-two per cent of the buildings suffered from moderate to heavy damage. In addition, the facilities in many of these apartments were at the same technological level as they had been during the early 20th century: nearly 95% of the apartments were heated by coal while approximately 79% still had toilets »on the half-stair.« It is a significant sign of change that only ten years later one must explain the meaning of this expression to younger people. Attending to the urge »to go,« entailed leaving the apartment, walking half a floor downstairs, entering a chamber that was unheated even during the winter, and so on …

15

IN DER BUNTEN REPUBLIK NEUSTADT
Entering the Colored Republic*

*The official name of the German state is »Bundesrepublik« (Federal Republic); changing two letters and inserting a space turns it into »Bunte Republik« (Colored Republic).

Früher fühlten sich die Neustädter vom Staat etwas vernachlässigt. Ein anonym bleiben wollender Dichter reimte 1912 im »Lokalanzeiger für Dresden=Neustadt«: »Die Neustadt zahlt Steuern / Wie's üblich ist und recht / Nur ist die Behandlung / Dafür oft gar schlecht.« Noch heute identifizieren Einwohner wie Touristen Dresden eher mit der Leere um Altmarkt und Neumarkt, in die sich Herders berühmtes »Elbflorenz« leichter hineinphantasieren läßt, als mit der weitgehend erhaltenen Neustadt.

Heute haben die Neustädter gelernt, daß es sich mit dieser Ignoranz ganz gut leben läßt. Abseits ambitionierter Stadtentwicklungskonzepte und hochsubventionierter Repräsentationskultur blüht die phantasievolle Eigeninitiative. Während der Zeit der DDR war die Neustadt sicher kein Widerstandsnest, wohl aber ein Refugium für alternative Lebensentwürfe. Vor allem Künstler und Intellektuelle, aber auch Arbeiter und kleine Angestellte ließen hier den greisen Herrscher im fernen Berlin einen guten Mann sein.

Daran ließ sich anknüpfen. Noch Ende 1989 schossen die ersten Bars, Cafés und Clubs aus dem Boden wie die sprichwörtlichen Pilze. Heute sind es weit mehr als 100, vom schummrigen Szenecafé über die urige Künstlerkneipe bis zur durchgestylten Cocktailbar. Für jeden Geschmack findet sich etwas: italienisch, spanisch, russisch, amerikanisch, französisch, wienerisch, türkisch, arabisch, asiatisch, sogar deutsch. Im Juni 1990 wurde zum ersten Mal die »Bunte Republik Neustadt« proklamiert, das dreitägige und weitgehend improvisierte Straßenfest der Neustädter und ihrer Gäste, an dem zuletzt über 100.000 Besucher teilnahmen.

Throughout history, the inhabitants of the Neustadt have often felt neglected. In 1912, an anonymous poet made the following complaint in a local newspaper: »Die Neustadt zahlt Steuern / Wie's üblich ist und recht / Nur ist die Behandlung / Dafür oft gar schlecht.« (The Neustadt pays taxes / as is common and the law / but the treatment it receives / is often very poor.) Indeed, even the inhabitants of Dresden, as well as the tourists who come here, tend to identify the city with the fragments of town which surround the former market squares, where they can imagine the so-called »Florence on the Elbe« filling the empty spaces, instead of with the well-preserved Neustadt.

The difference today is that people in the Neustadt have learned to live with being ignored. Distanced from ambitious town development projects and state-supported high culture, it is possible for one's own initiative to bloom. During the time of the GDR, the Neustadt was not a center of resistance at all, but instead a refuge for people who wanted to live life on their own terms. The artists, intellectuals, workers and employees who lived here simply let the old rulers in far-away Berlin carry on with their own lives. Following the transition, this provided a good basis for a new beginning. By the end of 1989, the first bars, cafés and clubs had already mushroomed up in the Neustadt. Today they number over one hundred, running the gamut from the dim cafés where the »underground artists« gather, to stylish cocktail bars. There is a place to suit every taste: Italian, Spanish, Russian, American, French, Viennese, Turkish, Arab, Asian, and even German. In June 1990 the »Bunte Republik« Neustadt was proclaimed for the first time. Since then, inhabitants and guests have commemorated this event every June with a three-day long street festival.

SPANIEN IN DER NEUSTADT
Spain in the Neustadt

Die Neustadt führt ein Doppelleben: brav und bürgerfleißig am Tage, ausschweifend und extravagant in der Nacht. In der Kunsthofpassage gibt sie sich spanisch: Von der urigen Tapasbar »El perro borracho« (»Der betrunkene Hund«) im Hof der Fabelwesen bis zum modernen spanischen Szenelokal »Copas y Tapas« im Hof der Metamorphosen. Und wieder zurück…

The Neustadt leads a double life: industrious, responsible, and civic-minded at dawn, unbridled and extravagant at night. Nightlife in the Kunsthof Passage follows the Spanish example. From the earthy Tapas bar »El Perro Borracho« (»The Drunken Dog«) in the Courtyard of the Fabulous Creatures, to the modern Spanish café and cocktail bar »Copas y Tapas« in the Courtyard of the Metamorphoses, and back.

HOF DER FABELWESEN
Courtyard of the Fabulous Creatures

In einem Märchen des romantischen Dichters E. T. A. Hoffmann tritt der Student Anselmus durch die Pforte eines Dresdner Bürgerhauses und befindet sich plötzlich im fabelhaften Reich eines Salamanders. Märchenhaft? Durchaus nicht. Allenfalls ein neuer Beweis für die prophetischen Gaben der Dichter…

According to a fairytale by German romanticist E. T. A. Hoffmann, the student Anselmus enters a residential house in Dresden and finds himself transported to the fabulous world of a salamander. Just a fairytale? Not at all … only one more piece of evidence that poets can be prophets …

Wer durch den Tordurchgang des denkmalgeschützten Bürgerhauses in der Alaunstraße 70 tritt, soll »sanft verwandelt werden«, wünscht sich die Künstlerin Viola Schöpe: Nicht einfach nur bezaubert, sondern verzaubert vom gehetzten und hetzenden Großstadtbewohner oder -touristen zu einem Menschen, der sich seiner »ursprünglichen schöpferischen Kräfte« wieder bewußt wird. Und vielleicht, wenn man sich wirklich darauf einläßt wie Hoffmanns Student Anselmus …

Aber auch prosaische Geister werden anerkennen müssen, daß hier ein enger und dunkler Hinterhof verwandelt wurde in einen bezaubernden Ort, der zum Flanieren und zum Verweilen einlädt. Und in dem man Entdeckungen machen kann beim schweifenden Betrachten und lustvollen ›Entschlüsseln‹ der detailreichen Fassadengestaltung.

Anyone who passes through the gate of the protected residential house at Alaunstraße 70 will be »tenderly changed.« Or at least that is the hope of artist Viola Schöpe. The visitor should not only be enchanted but transformed, from a hunted and haunting city dweller or tourist into a being »in tune with his or her innate creative energies.« And, perhaps, if one really dedicates him or herself as the student from Hoffmann's fairytale did …

Nevertheless, even less poetic types must admit that the once narrow and dark backyard has been transformed into an enchanting place that invites strolling and lingering, where one might discover surprising things by simply looking at or perhaps »interpreting« the detailed paintings on the walls.

Auf der südlichen Fassade (Rückwand des Nachbarhauses) befindet sich der Fluß, den Fluß des Lebens symbolisierend, das fließende Element des Wandels.

Jeder ist in seinem Boot auf dem Lebensweg im großen Lebensfluß. Jeder hat seine eigene Vorstellung von diesem Weg. Abhängigkeit ergibt sich aus der Absurdität der mitgenommenen Dinge. Was ist wirklich wichtig?

Die Leichtigkeit des Seins: Schwebende Figuren und Vögel, die sich aufschwingen, um in der Ferne Erfahrungen zu sammeln, nehmen den Blick des Betrachters mit in die Höhen der Träume.

Die Rückwand des Vorderhauses zeigt das Miteinanderleben und die Absicht, die Dinge mit einer guten Schwingung zu beleben. Der Musiker spielt auf einer Flöte. Die Tänzerin bezwingt den Haß durch den Tanz auf der Spirale. Der Lauscher reckt sich neugierig zum Nachbarn. So beginnt das Haus sich mit Tönen zu beleben.

Das Schiff über dem Eingang befindet sich über dem Menschenstrom. So wird der Durchgang zum Lebensfluß. Die Stille sitzt im Boot und das rote Tier beobachtet das Treiben.

On the southern wall of the house flows a river which symbolizes life and the fluid nature of its changes.

We must all make our own way in a boat through life. Each of us has a unique conception of this way and must learn how to overcome the absurd obstacles that may lie along this path. What is really important?

The ease of being: gliding figures and birds swing upwards, making these experiences seem far from home and taking the viewer into the heights of dreams.

The back wall of the house at Alaunstraße 70 depicts communal life and the aim to stimulate things with good vibrations. The musician plays the flute while the dancer transcends hate by dancing on the spiral. The listener cranes his neck to see his neighbor. The house is gradually stimulated.

The boat above the entrance follows the stream of people who passing through, thereby making this gate the river of life. Silence sits inside the boat, while the red animal observes all of the hustle and bustle.

Die nördliche Fassade führt ins Astralreich der höheren Energien, kosmischen Elemente, Sterne und Kometen. Gott und Göttin schleudern Blitze in den Himmel.

Der Kuß des Muttertiers mit den zum Himmel aufragenden, goldenen Hörnern symbolisiert die Liebe. Hier taucht die Liebe als das alles durchdringende Element auf, das das Universum zusammenhält. Heilende Energien wirken harmonisierend.

Das umgekehrte Tier hebt für einen Moment die Schwerkraft auf und läßt die physische Realität zurück, um andere Sphären zu erkennen.

Fliegende Fische verbinden das Element des Wassers mit der Luft.

Die Tänzerin am linken Ende der Wand gibt den Weg frei.

Die Spirale dreht sich noch einmal im Körper der Eisenskulptur hinauf und setzt Energien frei, die Trance.

Der Schamane Nanabusch sitzt friedlich in seinem Boot. Er symbolisiert den geistigen Ratgeber und wird von seinem Helfer, dem Elch, als Totem begleitet.

Die Überfahrt geht weiter. Die rote Schlange windet sich um die Säule zum Durchgang. Im Schatten lauert das blaue Schlangenkind.

Wellen und Wirbel führen sanft in den nächsten Hof.

(Viola Schöpe)

The northern facade leads into the divine empire. The male and female gods hurl flashes into heaven.

The kiss of the mother animal with the golden horns that reach into heaven symbolizes love. Here love is the omnipresent element that holds the universe together. Healing energies create harmony.

An inverted mirror image of the mother animal neutralizes gravity for a brief moment, making a break from physical reality in order to draw attention to other spheres.

Flying fish connect the elements of water and air.

The dancer on the left side of the wall opens the way.

Within the body of the metal sculpture, the spiral twists once again and releases more energy, pulling things into a trance.

The shaman Nanabusch sits peacefully in the boat. He represents the spiritual adviser and is accompanied by his assistant the Elk, who is the totem.

The scene continues. The red snake winds itself around the column near the back entrance, while the blue child of the snake lurks in the shadows.

Weaves and whirls lead into the next courtyard.

(Viola Schöpe)

DIE KÜNSTLERIN
The Artist

Viola Schöpe spricht gern über ihre Kunstwerke und doch wieder nicht.

Einerseits läßt es sich herrlich ›philosophieren‹ mit ihr, andererseits kann es schon mal vorkommen, daß sie eine mit einem Interview beauftragte Gymnasiastin auffordert, die vorbereiteten Fragen erst einmal selbst zu beantworten. Am liebsten hat es Viola Schöpe, wenn ihre Kunstwerke selbst sprechen, wenn sie es sind, die den Betrachter verwandeln (und nicht das Reden über Kunst).

Wenn man trotzdem einige charakteristische Aspekte ihrer Arbeitsweise herausgreifen möchte, dann vielleicht zuallererst, daß sie sich von den vielen mythologischen Anregungen inspirieren läßt, denen sie auf ihren Reisen durch Frankreich, Portugal, Nord- und Südamerika begegnet. Deren Synthese ist freilich die Leistung ihrer ganz individuellen Phantasie: Da bekommt der nordamerikanische Schamane auch schon mal einen skandinavischen Elch zum Begleiter.

Offenbar ist auch ihre perfektionistische Liebe zum Material: Als Bühnenbildnerin hatte sie immer damit zu kämpfen, daß am Theater alles ›schöner Schein‹ ist. Im »Hof der Fabelwesen« dagegen ist alles ›echt‹: Nach wenigen Vorstudien (Wie hätte sich eine solche Arbeit auch simulieren lassen?) kratzte sie ihre Figuren direkt in den noch feuchten Putz. Eine ungeheure Herausforderung, allein wenn man bedenkt, daß 900 m² Wandfläche zu gestalten waren, darunter die schier endlose, fast ungegliederte und zu allem Überfluß nach Norden weisende Rückwand des Nachbargebäudes.

Die Ornamentfliesen hat Viola Schöpe in portugiesischen Manufakturen ausgewählt und im Handgepäck nach Dresden transportiert, die roten und blauen stammen aus Italien, die goldenen wurden eigens für den Kunsthof in Meißen gebrannt.

Die Sandsteinfiguren sind in Fundstücke aus der Neustadt gehauen. So haben Schöpes Figuren immer eine doppelte Geschichte: eine mythologische und eine materielle.

Viola Schöpe
geboren 1963 in Gera, nach dem Studium an der Hochschule für Bildende Künste in Dresden (1983-88) Bühnen- und Kostümbildnerin in Schwerin, lebt seit 1990 als freischaffende Malerin und Plastikerin abwechselnd in Dresden und Angers, unterbrochen von regelmäßigen Studienaufenthalten in Portugal, Brasilien, Nordamerika, Afrika, ...

Viola Schöpe
was born in 1963 in Gera, Thuringia. Following her studies at the Academy of Fine Arts (HfBK) in Dresden (1983-88), she worked as a set designer in Schwerin. Since 1990, she has made a living as a freelance painter and sculptor, dividing her time between Dresden and Angers, France, when not on sabbatical in Portugal, Brazil, North America, or Africa.

Viola Schöpe loves to talk about her works but at the same time often seems reluctant. On one hand, it is possible to »philosophize« with her, on the other she once made a student interviewer go home and answer the questions she had prepared for the artist herself before she would agree to answer them. Schöpe likes her creatures to speak for themselves and prefers works of art to transform people, not the discourse regarding them.

If one nevertheless tries to discuss some of the important aspects of her work with her, he or she must begin with the role of mythology. Schöpe traveled extensively through France, Portugal, North and South America, always paying close attention to the mythological narratives of each place and later adapting them into her own interpretations. The shaman Nanabusch, who originates in North American Indian folklore, and his assistant the Elk, taken from Northern European mythology, are examples.

Schöpe's perfectionist affection for materials is obvious. Working as a stage designer, she always suffered when making virtual things. In the Courtyard of the Fabulous Creatures, everything is real. After making only a few sketches, she carved the figures directly into wet plaster. A significant challenge when one takes into account that she had 900 square meters (approximately 9.700 square feet) of wall to work with, which included one dark, virtually uninterrupted facade of the neighbor's house.

Schöpe selected the ornamental tiles herself from Portuguese factories and brought them back to Germany as hand luggage. The red and the blue tiles were imported from Italy, while the golden ones were specially made for the Kunsthof in the famous porcelain manufactory in Meißen. The sandstone figures were made from carved stones that were found in the Neustadt. Thus, every figure has a double history: a mythical one and a material one.

DER GINKGOBAUM
The Ginkgo-Tree

Der Ginkgo ist das Symbol der Kunsthofpassage. Nicht nur weil er sich als Überlebenskünstler seit 250 Millionen Jahren allen Veränderungen anpaßt und doch immer derselbe bleibt. Seine »zweihäusigen«, fächerförmigen Blätter eignen sich überdies vorzüglich, der oder dem Geliebten »geheimen Sinn« zu kosten zu geben. Sagt der Dichter.

The Ginkgo-tree is the symbol of Kunsthof Passage. It has been selected as such not only for its repute as a »survival artist« that has managed to adapt itself to an ever-changing environment for over 250 million years, but also for its constancy; despite all of the changes it has undergone, it nevertheless remains the same. Furthermore, its »two-lobed«, fan-shaped leaves are a sensual delicacy, to give one's lover a »secret sense« to taste. The poet says–.

Ginkgo Biloba

Dieses Baumes Blatt, der von Osten
Meinem Garten anvertraut,
Gibt geheimen Sinn zu kosten,
Wie's den Wissenden erbaut.

Ist es ein lebendig Wesen,
Das sich in sich selbst getrennt?
Sind es zwei, die sich erlesen,
Daß man sie als eines kennt?

Solche Fragen zu erwidern
Fand ich wohl den rechten Sinn.
Spürst du nicht an meinen Liedern,
Daß ich eins und doppelt bin?

(Johann Wolfgang von Goethe)

Ginkgo Biloba

This tree's leaf that from the East
To my garden's been entrusted
Holds a secret sense, and grist
To a man intent on knowledge.

Is it one, this thing alive,
By and in itself divided,
Or two beings who connive
That as one the world shall see them?

Fitly now I can reveal
What the pondered question taught me;
In my songs do you not feel
That at once I'm one and double?

(Johann Wolfgang von Goethe,
translated by Michael Hamburger)

HOF DES LICHTS » » » » » » » » » » »
Courtyard of Light

»Es werde Licht.« Auch ganz gewöhnliche Sterbliche mußten zwangsläufig auf diese göttliche Idee verfallen, wenn sie sich bis 1997 in den heutigen »Hof des Lichts« verirrten (was zum Glück selten vorkam). Dieser Hinterhof war – kurz gesagt – ein besonders dunkles Loch. Bis es Licht ward, dauerte es in diesem Falle allerdings ein paar Tage …

»Let there be light.« Even ordinary mortals were struck with this divine idea when, for some odd reason, they chanced upon what has been transformed into today's »Courtyard of Light.« (Fortunately this did not happen very often.) Previously, this yard was, in simple terms, little more than a dark hole. Thus, in the case of this courtyard, the trajectory from concept to finished product spanned a number of days …

Mit dem 1998 begonnenen Hof des Lichts wurde der Kunsthof zur Kunsthofpassage. Anders als beim bereits fertiggestellten Hof der Fabelwesen wurde die künstlerische Gestaltung für die 1998 hinzugekommenen Höfe in einem nationalen Wettbewerb ausgeschrieben. Die Entwürfe konnten vier Wochen lang im Gebäude des ehemaligen VEB Landmaschinenbau »Fortschritt« (heute »Mrs. Hippie« im Hof des Lichts) begutachtet werden. Die Wettbewerbssieger wurden schließlich – ein für künstlerische Gestaltungen einmaliger (und zugegeben risikoreicher) Vorgang – in einem demokratischen Votum bestimmt.

With the 1998-9 reconstruction of the Courtyard of Light, the Kunsthof became the Kunsthof Passage. Unlike the already finished Courtyard of the Fabulous Creatures, the artistic designs for the courtyards added after 1998 were the subject of a national competition. Drafts for the courtyards were put on public display for four weeks, inside a building in the Courtyard of Light which used to be the VEB Landmaschinenbau »Fortschritt«*, and which now houses the fashion store »Mrs Hippie«. The winners of the competition were determined by a democratic vote—a unique and risky method of selection in the field of art.

* Literally: a people-owned factory called *Progress* that manufactured agricultural machinery.

Der Hof des Lichts ist auf den ersten Blick der unspektakulärste der Kunsthöfe und doch der, der dem Grundkonzept der Kunsthofpassage, nicht Museum zu sein, sondern eine Bühne für lebendige Kunst, am meisten entspricht. Hier wurden mit zwei Stegbühnen und mehreren Projektionsflächen vor allem Räume und Möglichkeiten für temporäre Multimedia-Performances und Installationen, Filmprojektionen und Action-Theater geschaffen.

At first glance, the Yard of Light appears less spectacular than the other courtyards. Nevertheless, it is the one that embodies the concept behind the Kunsthof Passage best. Here artists from abroad get a chance to experiment with light and space. It is not an open air museum but rather a venue for performances, temporary installations, movie presentations, and live theatre.

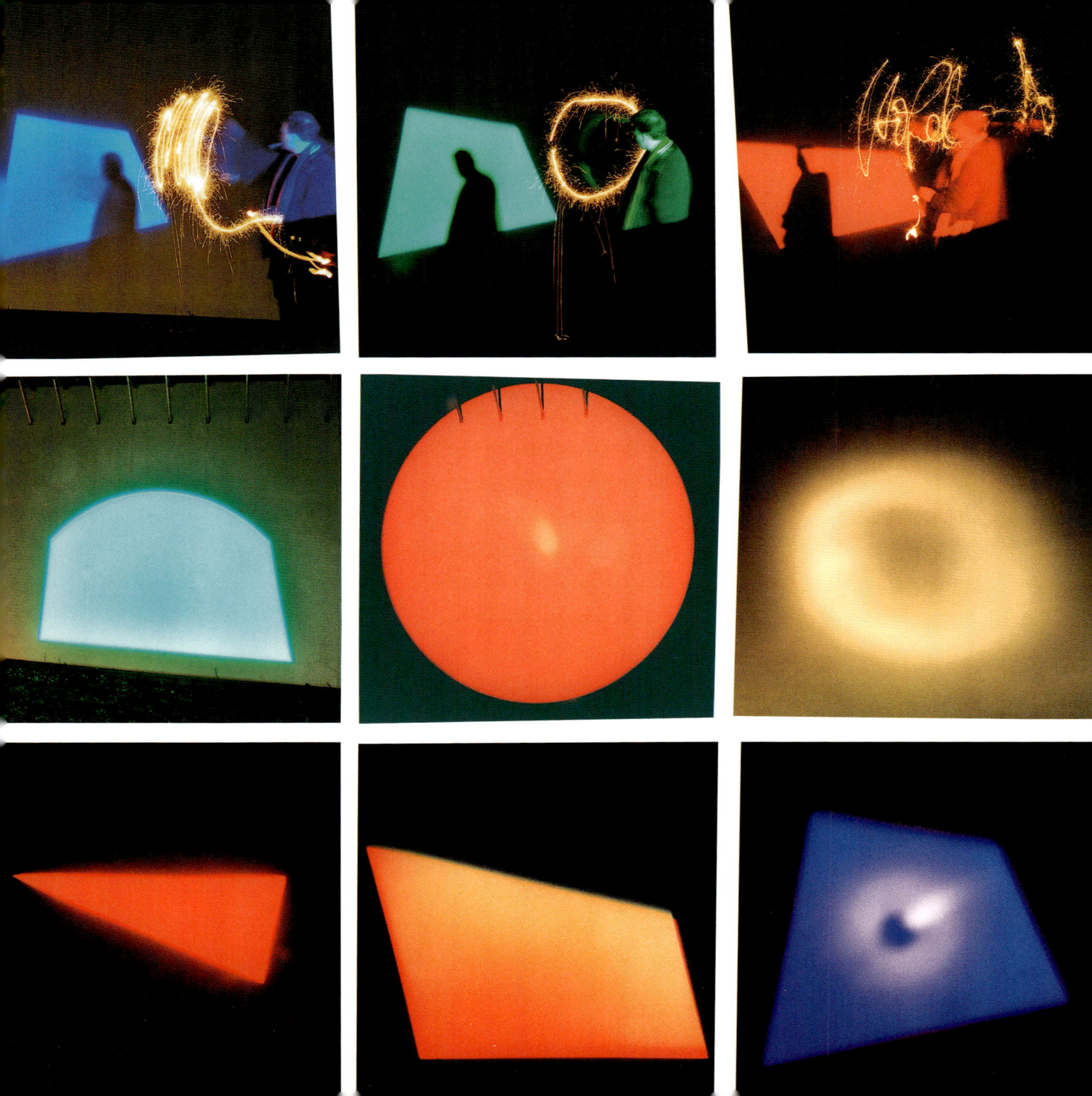

Vor der Rekonstruktion zeichnete sich der enge, von allen Seiten durch hohe, halbverfallene Mauern begrenzte Hof durch eine besonders unwirtliche Düsternis aus. Also wurden bei der Gebäudesanierung ausschließlich helle Farben verwendet und überdies große Metallspiegel montiert, die das Sonnenlicht in den Hof reflektieren. Der Kunsthof wäre freilich kein Kunsthof, wenn diese Spiegel den Hof »einfach nur so« erhellten. Vielmehr erzeugen sie je nach Sonnenstand vielfältige farbige Reflexe auf Wänden und Pflaster.

Prior to reconstruction, the narrow yard was enclosed by tall, crumbling walls, and was plagued with an inhospitable obscurity. For these reasons, only light colors were employed in the reconstruction of this yard, and to garner as much natural light as possible, mirrors were installed to reflect the sun. However, the Kunsthof would not be the Kunsthof if the purpose behind the mirrors were limited to a single technical function. In addition, the mirrors produce multi-colored patterns on the walls and pavement.

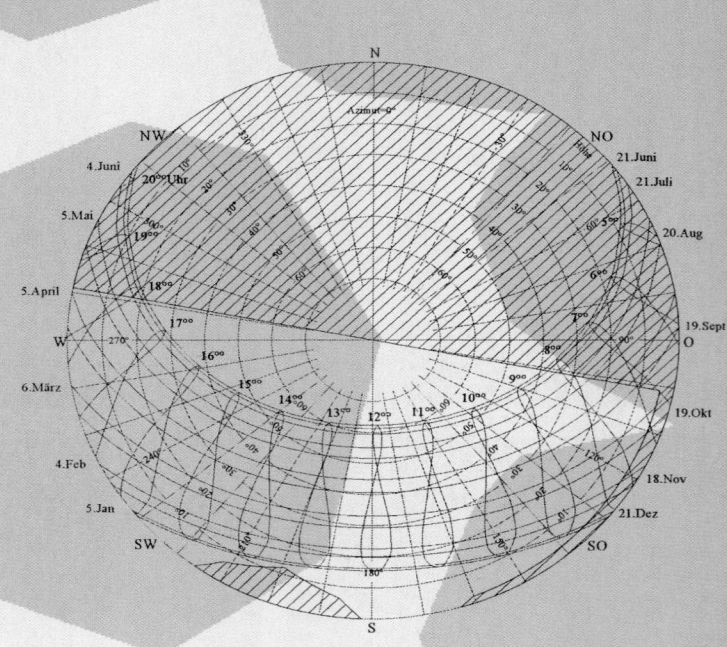

Eine gleichsam »verkehrte« Sonnenuhr zeigt die Zeit nicht durch Schattenwurf, sondern durch Lichteinfall an.

An inverted sundial indicates the time, not through the shadow it casts, but through the incidence of light which falls upon it.

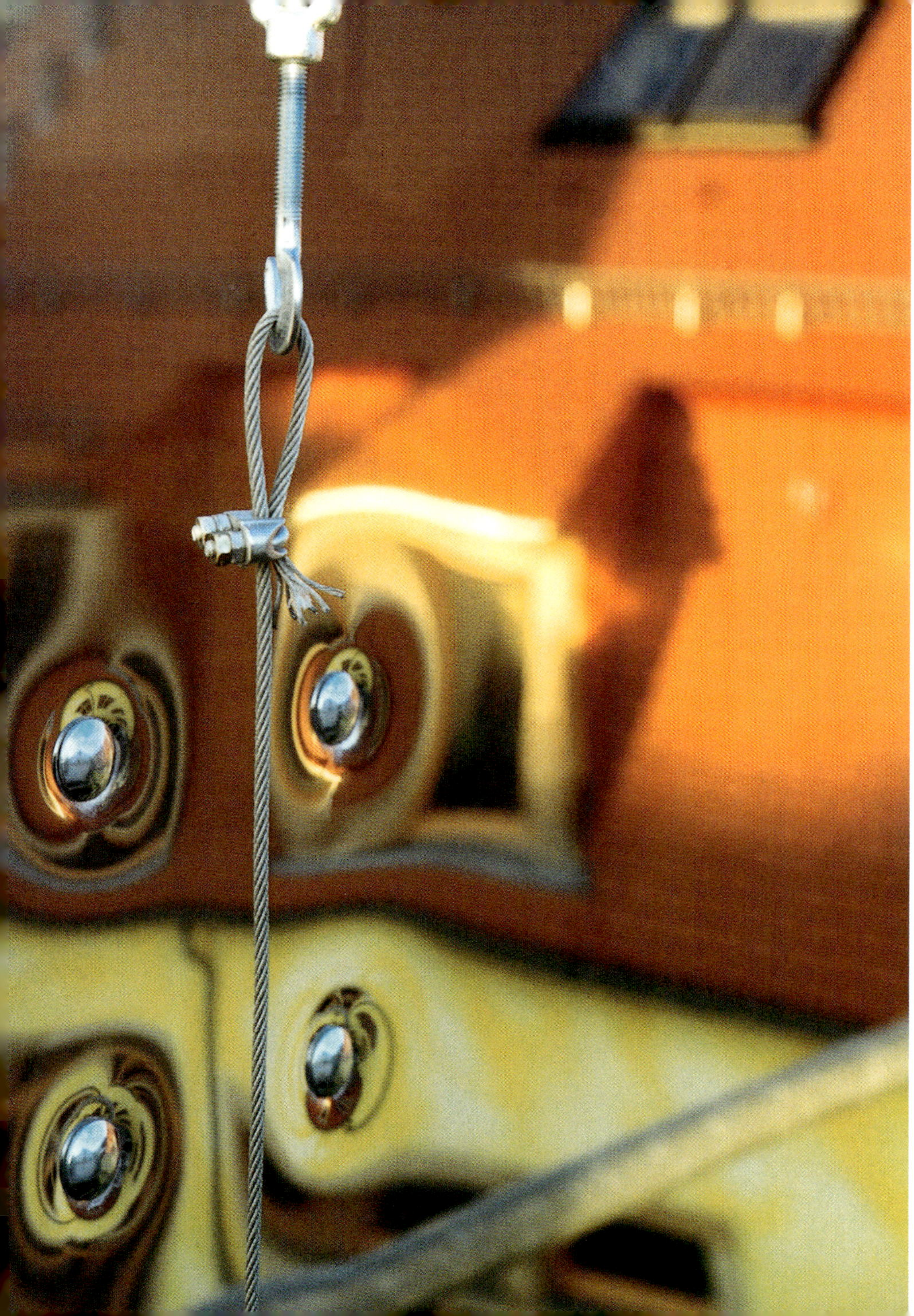
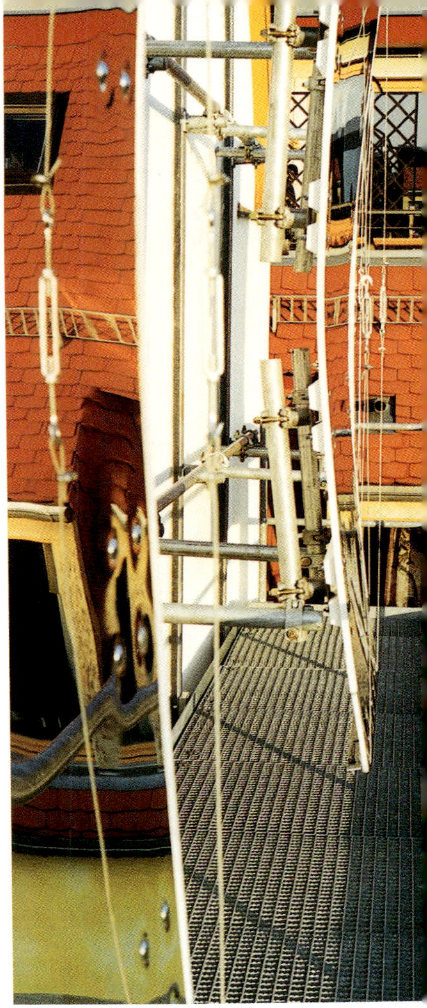
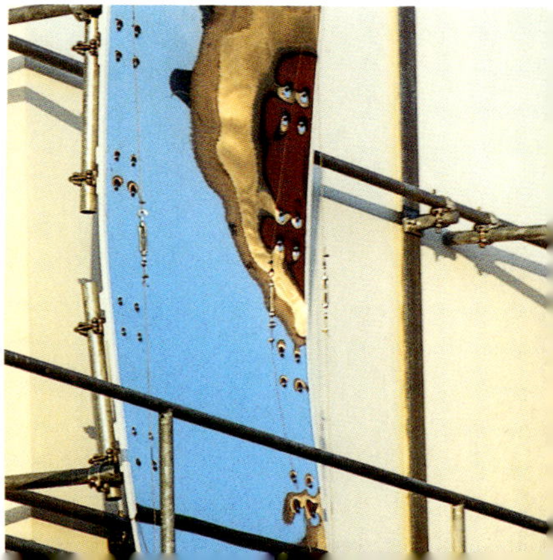

DIE BEWOHNER ALS »PLANUNGSZIEL«
Interview mit dem Geschäftsführer der Ginkgo Projektentwicklung, Tankred Lenz

Residents as a »planning objective.«
Interview with the Manager of Ginkgo Project Development, Tankred Lenz

Herr Lenz, die Projekte Ihrer Ginkgo Projektentwicklung sind »etwas anders«…

Tankred Lenz (TL): Das mag daran liegen, daß für uns die Altbaumodernisierung sich nicht darauf beschränkt, die Bauhülle und die Technik auf ein modernes Niveau zu bringen. Vielmehr sind die in diesen Bauten lebenden Menschen mit ihren Wünschen nach neuen Entdeckungen und Gefühlen unser »Planungsziel«. Das Lebensumfeld, die Wohnungen, Balkone, Höfe, Dächer und Fassaden müssen ansprechen und möglichst zu eigener Kreativität anregen.

Besonders der erste der Kunsthöfe, der Hof der Fabelwesen, erinnert wahrscheinlich nicht zufällig an eine mediterrane Szenerie.

TL: Ich habe vier Jahre in Madrid verbracht und Lebenslust und Stil der Spanier erfahren. Der erste Hof sollte mir auch als Haltepunkt in meiner neuen Heimat Sachsen helfen. In Barcelona kam ich außerdem mit den Bauwerken Antoni Gaudís in Kontakt, die mich in ihrer Kühnheit und Perfektion nachhaltig inspiriert haben. Aber die Höfe der Kunsthofpassage sind ja nicht mein »Werk«, sondern Ergebnisse vielfältiger Dialoge zwischen den Künstlern, ihren Helfern, den Planern und uns.

Es ist leider nicht alltäglich, daß Kunst als integraler Bestandteil einer Bauaufgabe gesehen wird.

TL: Kunst am Bau gibt es seit den alten Ägyptern und prähistorischen Höhlenmalereien. In der in der Neustadt besonders präsenten Gründerzeit und im Jugendstil erlebte sie neue Höhepunkte, die sich tatsächlich in der Sachlichkeit der Moderne stark verloren haben. Vielleicht ist es gerade deshalb an der Zeit,

Mr. Lenz, the projects of Ginkgo always seem to take an unconventional approach.

Tankred Lenz (TL): For us, the modernization of old buildings does not simply mean bringing the exteriors of the buildings and techniques used in their reconstruction into the modern age. Instead, we consider the wishes of the buildings' inhabitants to be our »planning objective.« In order to fulfill this objective, the living environment of the apartments—the terraces, courtyards, roofs, and facades—must appeal to the people living in them and at the same time stimulate their own sense of creativity.

The first of the Kunsthof courtyards, the Courtyard of the Fabulous Creatures, in particular, is reminiscent of scenery on the Mediterranean.

TL: I lived in Madrid for four years and became enamored of the Spanish lifestyle. The first courtyard of the Kunsthof has helped me readjust to my new home in Saxony by reminding me of what I experienced in Madrid. In addition, while in Barcelona I visited the buildings of Antoni Gaudí and was impressed by their boldness and perfect balance. Nevertheless, the Kunsthof Passage is not solely a product of my own conception, but instead is the result of the dialog among the artists, their assistants, the designers, and Ginkgo Project Management.

How you came to look upon Art as essential piece of your building projects?

TL: Architectural art has existed since the time of the Egyptians and prehistoric cave paintings. During the periods of the »Founder's Years« and Art Deco, architectural art reached new climaxes, only later to disappe-

Kunst wieder als Bestandteil von Architektur und nicht nur als Ausstattungsgegenstand zu verstehen.

Darf man Sie – besonders in diesem Zusammenhang – nach weiteren Plänen fragen?

TL: Ein weiterer Kunsthof, der »Hof der Tiere«, ist im Bau. Er soll sich um die Themen ›primitive‹ Natur, Tiere und sächsische Steinmetzkunst bewegen. Ein anderes interessantes Projekt beschäftigt sich mit der Umnutzung schöner Industriedenkmäler der Jahrhundertwende zu Büros und Wohnungen, sogenannten Lofts.

ar in the functionalism of Modernism. But I think it is about time to begin understanding art as an integral component of architecture and not just as »fixture«.

Continuing along this line, may I ask you about any future plans for the Kunsthof?

TL: Another courtyard is currently under construction. We have tentatively named it the »Courtyard of the Animals.« It will deal with ›primitive‹ themes: nature, animals, and Saxon stone-cutter art. Another interesting project involves the remodeling of some beautiful old industrial buildings from the early 1900s into offices and lofts.

HOF DER METAMORPHOSEN » » » » » » »
Courtyard of the Metamorphoses

Nichts bleibt wie es war – wer wüßte das besser als die Ostdeutschen, die 1989 erleben (und ein wenig mithelfen) durften, daß ein System verschwand, dessen Repräsentanten die »historische Wahrheit« auf ihrer Seite wähnten. Freilich vollziehen sich die meisten Veränderungen subtiler. Wer den Hof der Metamorphosen besucht, sollte deshalb etwas mehr Zeit mitbringen und etwas genauer hinschauen.

Nothing lasts forever. Who could possibly know this better than the East Germans, who witnessed the abrupt dismantling of a political system once thought to be invincible. Most transitions are much more subtle, however. That is precisely why one should take time when visiting the Courtyard of the Metamorphoses.

41

Sprachlos und kalt wie archaische Wächter lehnen die sechs schmalen Schilde des Arend Zwicker an den Fassaden. Nicht einmal der Künstler selbst hat sie bislang zum Reden zu bringen vermocht – behauptet er jedenfalls. »Fremd, lässig und rätselhaft« stünden sie dort. Soviel allerdings steht fest: Als Zwicker 1998 mit der Arbeit am Hof der Metamorphosen begann, war der Hof der Fabelwesen bereits fertiggestellt und für ihn eine Herausforderung. Jeder Hof der Kunsthofpassage sollte eine eigene Welt sein und alle zusammen doch ein Ensemble. Also entschloß sich Zwicker, »seinen« Hof in bewußter Auseinandersetzung mit den anderen zu entwickeln. Er nennt das »harmonisierende Ästhetik durch kontrastintensive Gegensätzlichkeit«.

Soweit die Theorie. In der sogenannten Realität fällt vor der Harmonie die Gegensätzlichkeit der Gestaltungskonzeptionen ins Auge. Während Viola Schöpe in südländischer Farbigkeit schwelgt, beschränkt sich Zwicker auf kühle Noblesse. Während die Fabelwesen förmlich in den Putz eingekratzt sind, die Fassaden aufreißen und aus ihnen heraustreten, berühren die Stelen die Fassaden gleichsam scheu in je einem einzigen Punkt. Wenn sich das bei bis zu 15 Meter langen und tonnenschweren Metallstücken nicht verböte, könnte man vermuten: schüchtern oder zärtlich. Sie verraten es nicht.

Speechless and cold like archaic guards, the six slender shields made by Arend Zwicker lean against the facades. Not even the artist himself was able to bring them to speak. Instead, they simply lie in wait, »strange, nonchalant, and enigmatic.« At least one thing is for certain: when Zwicker started working on his courtyard, Viola Schöpe's Courtyard of the Fabulous Creatures was already finished and posed a certain challenge to him. Individually, each yard should exist as a separate world of its own, while all together, the different yards should form a stringent ensemble. With this in mind, Zwicker decided to create his yard in deliberate tackling with the others. He calls this principle »harmonizing aesthetics through intense contrasts.«

That's the theory. In so-called reality, the contrasts are much more obvious than the harmony. Unlike Schöpe, who favors Mediterranean colors, Zwicker reduces his composition to cool noblesse, and while the fabulous creatures are carved into the facades, tear them up, and break through them, Zwicker's metal steles touch the walls at a single point. If it were possible to say such things of pieces of steel 15 meters (~ 50 feet) in height, one might say that these particular pieces appear shy or tender. They disclose nothing.

Es gibt zwei Dinge, die man mit Papier nie tun sollte: es der Feuchtigkeit und dem Licht aussetzen. Grund genug, es trotzdem zu tun, befand Zwicker, wählte 24 verschiedene Papiere, tauchte sie je zur Hälfte in Leinöl und hängte sie als eine Art Langzeitversuch in kleinen Metallrahmen an die Außenwände der Gebäude im Hof der Metamorphosen. Der aufmerksame Betrachter kann die langsamen und sukzessiven Veränderungen des Papiers in der Sonne beobachten und die entstehenden und vergehenden Strukturen – ganz nach Gutdünken – als Zerstörung der Substanz begreifen, als ästhetisch reizvolle temporäre Kunstwerke oder als beides zugleich.

There are at least two things that one should never do with paper: 1) get it wet, and 2) leave it exposed to the sun. Two more reasons to do exactly that, thought Zwicker, who promptly selected 24 different papers, dipped half of each sheet in oil, and placed them in small metal frames which he hung on the walls of the houses of the courtyard. They have been displayed there as an ongoing experiment. The astute visitor can observe the slow transformation of the papers by the sun, and, as a personal matter of choice, can interpret this as the destruction of the material or see it as a fascinating work of art, or do both at the same time.

44

Die Stelen fertigte Zwicker gemeinsam mit der Metallwerkstatt Karlheinz Löffler. Anschließend wurden sie in 6 Meter langen Teilstücken in die Kunsthofpassage transportiert, montiert und mit zwei Flaschenzügen aufgerichtet. ›Metamorphose‹ scheint hier auf den ersten Blick ausschließlich Vergänglichkeit zu meinen: Schon wenige Wochen nach ihrer Installation waren die Plastiken verrostet. Der Schein trügt. Die Stelen bestehen aus einem verzinkten Stahlskelett, das mit einem Mantel aus Cortenstahlblech überzogen ist, einem Material, das eine oberflächliche Rostschicht bildet, die ähnlich wie Grünspan bei Kupfer die weitere Korrosion aufhält. In die gekrümmten Oberflächen sind Glasfaserbündel eingelassen, in die von verdeckt angebrachten Projektoren Licht eingespeist wird. In der Dämmerung verwandeln sich die metallenen Stelen langsam in feine Linien aus Licht, die sie noch höher erscheinen lassen als sie sind. Ergänzt und kontrastiert werden die Stahlskulpturen schließlich durch ein sich perspektivisch nach oben verjüngendes Seilsystem für Rankpflanzen.

Zwicker made the steles in collaboration with the metal manufacturer Karlheinz Löffler in Dresden. Pieces 6 meters in length were taken to the Kunsthof Passage, assembled, and erected using two blocks and pulleys. No more than a few weeks later, the sculptures already seemed to be rusting. Metamorphosis as transience? Appearances can be deceiving. The steles consist of a skeleton of galvanized steel covered with a layer of so-called »corten steel,« a type of metal, which not unlike copper, produces a thin coat of rust that protects the underlying metal from further corrosion. Thin bundles of glass have been attached to the uneven surface of the metal, and are illuminated at night. At dusk they transform the steles into fine beams of light that make them appear much taller than they actually are. The steel sculptures are complemented by a network of wires intended to hold tendril plants, that gradually gets smaller as it nears the top of the steles, in order to support the perspective.

DER KÜNSTLER
The Artist

Von der malerischen Arbeit – einer Komposition aus großen, starkfarbigen Putzflächen –, mit der Arend Zwicker den Wettbewerb zum »Hof der Metamorphosen« gewann, hat den eigentlichen Gestaltungsprozeß so gut wie nichts überdauert. Nur daß es dieser Hof sein sollte, der Zwicker wegen der Klarheit seiner Proportionen reizte, war von Anfang an klar. Architekturbezogene Kunst wird nicht am sprichwörtlichen Reißbrett entworfen und dann maßstäblich umgesetzt, sondern ist sinnliche und im Prozeß der Ausführung regelrecht physische Auseinandersetzung mit den vorgefundenen Volumen, Kubaturen, Räumen, Materialien, Flächen… Der studierte Maler und Grafiker Zwicker, der seit Anfang der 1990er Jahre »am Bau« arbeitet und unter anderem Restaurants in Berlin, die Versöhnungskirche Zwickau-Neuplanitz und das Kinder- und Jugendhaus Dresden-Gruna mit Kunstobjekten ausgestattet hat, weiß das natürlich und ist deshalb froh, daß Bauherr und Architekt »seines« Hofes geduldig zusahen, wie aus dem malerischen Entwurf zunächst ein grafischer und schließlich ein »statuarischer« (Zwicker) wurde. Im Verlaufe dieses Prozesses löste sich Zwicker in fortwährender künstlerischer Auseinandersetzung mit den Arbeiten Viola Schöpes von jeglicher, seine Malerei eigentlich kennzeichnenden Kleinteiligkeit, und – das klingt paradox, ist es aber nicht – reduzierte seinen Entwurf zu monumentaler Größe, wobei er sich mit Pragmatismus und Lakonie wirksam gegen Pathos imprägnierte.

Arend Zwicker
geboren 1958 in Chemnitz, nach dem Schulbesuch Lehre als Theatermaler und Studium der Malerei und Grafik an der Hochschule für Bildende Künste Dresden, seit 1988 freischaffend mit zahlreichen Ausstellungen im In- und Ausland, seit 1990 Planung und Ausführung architekturbezogener Projekte. Zwicker lebt in Dresden.

Arend Zwicker
was born in Chemnitz 1958, did an apprenticeship as theater painter, and then went on to study painting and drawing at the Academy of Fine Arts (HfBK) at Dresden. Starting in 1989, he has had a series of exhibitions in Germany and abroad, and since 1990 he has engaged in the design and execution of architectural art. He lives in Dresden.

Only a few things are left from the draft design that Arend Zwicker won the contest for the Courtyard of the Metamorphoses with. The only thing that was for sure all the time was that it had to be the back yard with simple proportions. Architectural art is not created on the drawing board and then transferred, scaled to life-size, but instead arises sometimes through physical confrontation with the actual volumes, spaces and materials.

Zwicker who started as painter and drawer knows this much, since he has worked in architecture since the early 1990s. Among the buildings that house his works are some bars and restaurants in Berlin, a church in Zwickau, and the youth center in Dresden-Gruna. Zwicker was more than happy that the owner and the architect did not complain when the plans for »his« courtyard changed from heavily-colored wall paintings to drawings and, later, to a »statuesque« (Zwicker) form. During this process Zwicker kept his critical attention focused on the work by Viola Schöpe. This time his work was detached from the detailed style that was typical for his paintings and drawings, instead exhibiting the new monumental style he developed. Nevertheless, he protected himself against false pathos with the help of laconism and pragmatism.

PFLANZEN IN DER KUNSTHOFPASSAGE
Plants in the Kunsthof Passage

»Es grient so grien, wenn Spaniens Bliehten bliehen.« Mal abgesehen vom beinahe sächsischen Wohllaut, ist dieser Operetten-Song zumindest im ›Spanien der Neustadt‹ nicht gänzlich sinnfrei. Pflanzen gibt es hier auch außerhalb der Blumenläden. Und wenn sie nicht zu abgegriffen wäre, könnte man hier die Metapher von der grünen Oase in der Steinwüste gebrauchen. (Tun wir aber nicht.) So ziemlich jeder erdenkliche Platz ist bepflanzt: die Dächer ›extensiv‹ (d. h. wassersparend) mit Lavendelheide oder, wo das baulich möglich ist, ›intensiv‹ mit Trogpflanzen und kleinwüchsigen Kiefern, die Fassaden mit Schlingern (Blauregen, Baumwürger), Rankern (verschiedenen Waldreben, besser bekannt als Clematis, Jungfernreben) und Spreizklimmern.
In den Höfen wurden, wenn möglich, Bäume gepflanzt. Das ist nützlich, weil die vielen Pflanzen Feuchtigkeit speichern, die Luft reinigen, Schatten spenden und Lärm schlucken. Und es grünt so grün.

In the Kunsthof Passage, plants are not strictly confined to flower shops but grow naturally and abundantly in the courtyards. In fact, if it were not already so hackneyed, one might use the metaphor of a green oasis in a stone desert to describe the Kunsthof Passage and its relationship with the rest of the Neustadt. (We do not, however). Flora abounds in everyimaginable place: lavender, a so-called »extensive« matter which serves as a water reserve, blankets the rooftops. Where possible, trough plants and small jaw grasses have been cultivated, covering the walls in a lattice comprised of the tendrils of various types of vines—blue rain, tree strangler, and those known scientifically by the name Clematis and more commonly as »Old Maid« vines.
In addition, trees have been planted where space has permitted. The plants serve a number of important purposes. They store moisture, purify the air, absorb noise, provide shade, and, perhaps most obvious, contribute to the ambience of each courtyard through their simple beauty.

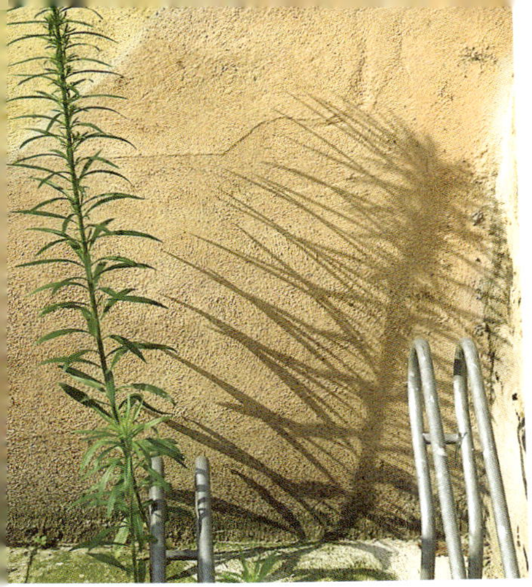
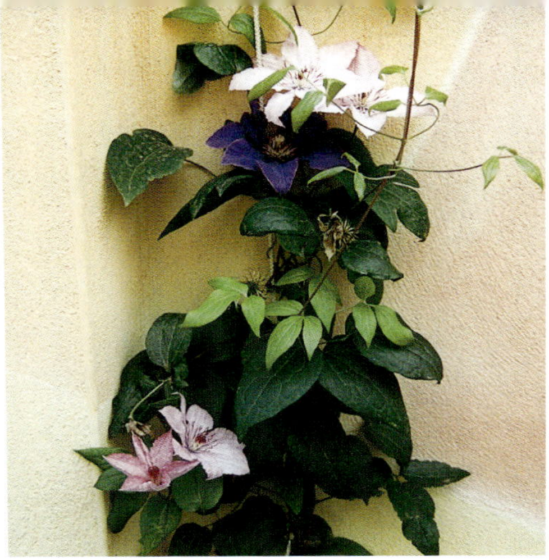
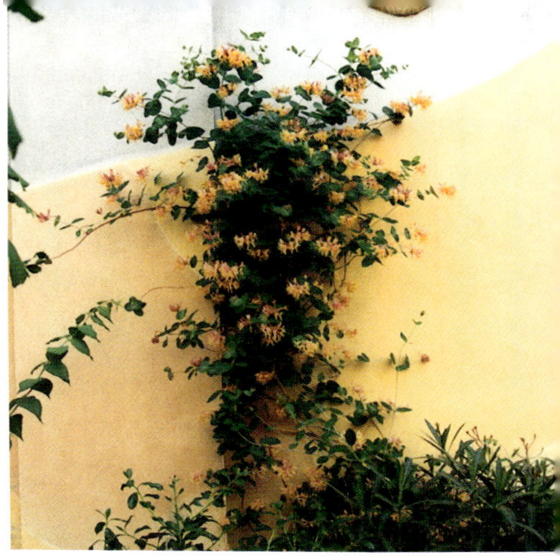
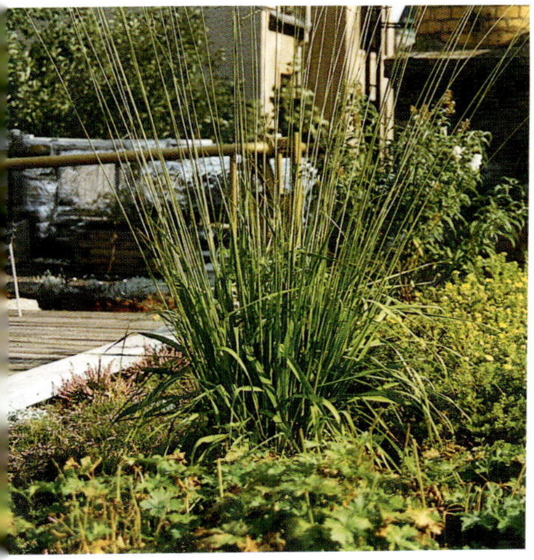
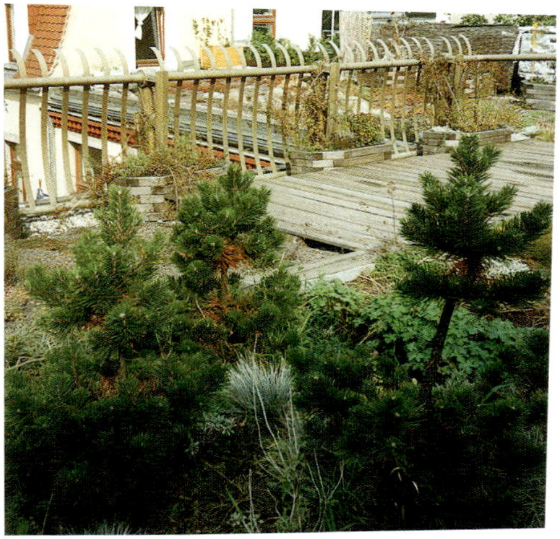
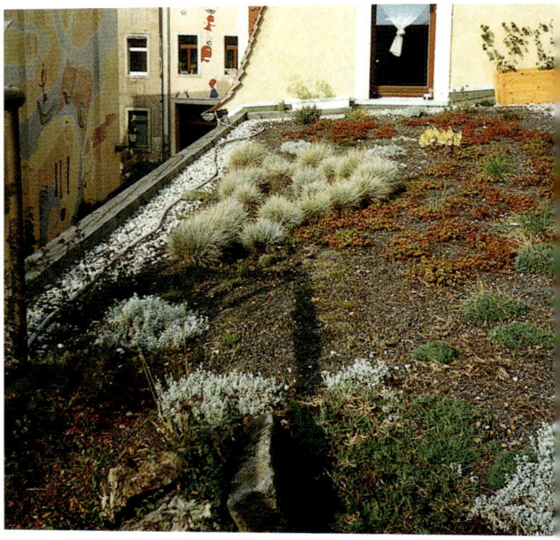
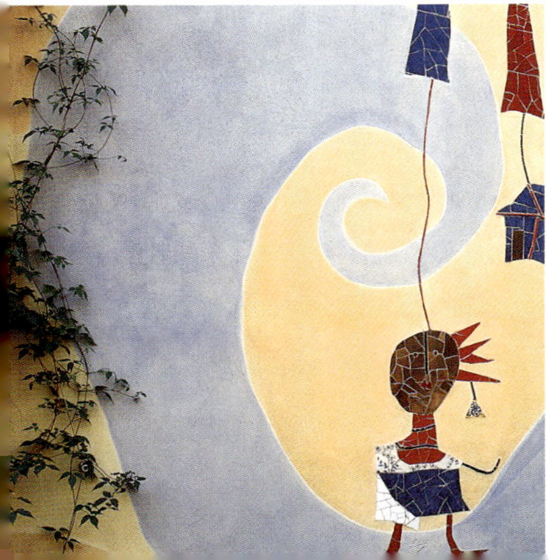
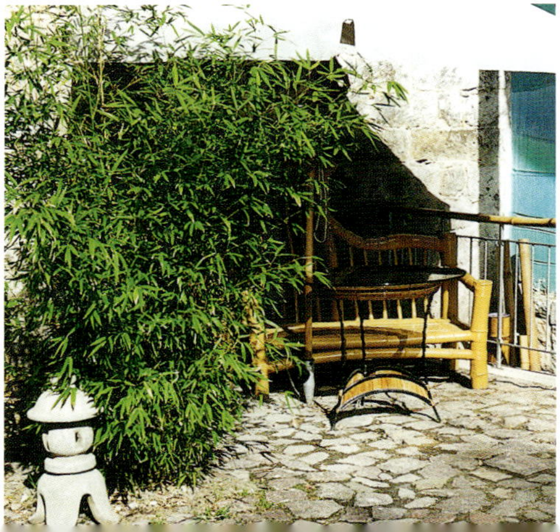
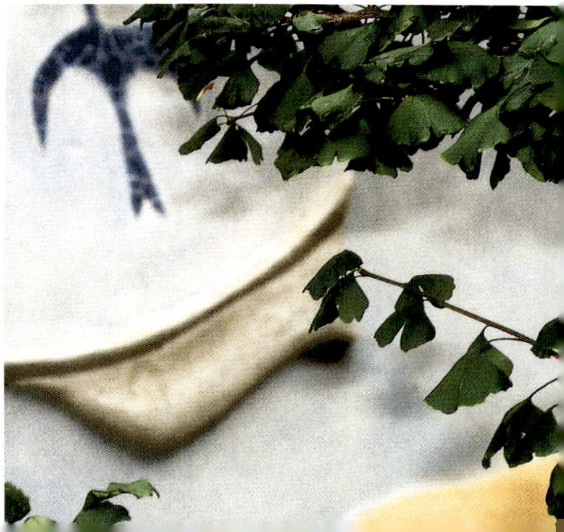

HOF DER ELEMENTE
Courtyard of the Elements

Was haben St. Petersburg, Dresden und Herrenchiemsee gemeinsam? – Regenrinnen. Wem diese Antwort etwas abwegig erscheint, der hat einerseits sicherlich recht, kennt andererseits die Geschichten nicht, die das sogenannte Leben schreibt ...

What does Dresden have in common with St. Petersburg in Russia and Herrenchiemsee in Bavaria? —Gutters. Whoever finds this to be strange may be right in doing so but does not really know the stories that have been written by life ...

51

52

Der Hof der Elemente könnte mit gleichem Recht »Hof der großen Kontraste« heißen. Einer meerblauen Fassade, an der absonderlich verschlungene Regenrohre emporranken, steht eine leuchtend sonnengelbe gegenüber, auf die wie hingeweht wirkende, goldfarbene Alu-Bleche montiert sind. Zwischen beiden scheinen die Farben sich im Grün steiler Grashügel zu vermischen. Bei Regen – während der Sommerzeit auch tagsüber zu jeder halben Stunde – wird dieses farbenfrohe Architekturschauspiel zum Konzert. Das Wasser macht dann die Musik. Gluckst in den Fallrohren, braust über die Kaskaden, rauscht in die Trichter, rumort in der Trompete und tröpfelt zuerst leise aus den Öffnungen des unteren Trichters, bis es später in dicken Strahlen hervorsprudelt. Wann hat man sich je zuvor gewünscht, im Regen zu stehen?

Die Fassade auf der Westseite des Hofes betrachtet man hingegen am besten vormittags bei Sonnenschein, wenn die Metall-Lamellen ein graziöses Licht-Schatten-Spiel auf Fassaden und Pflaster zaubern.

The Courtyard of the Elements may just as well be called the Courtyard of Huge Contrasts. An ocean-blue facade crawling with bizarre gutters on the right-hand side of the courtyard faces a sun-yellow wall to the left, with golden plates that appear blown to the surface. These colors mingle with the green of the steep grass hills that fill the space in between. When it rains (during the summer it »rains« twice hourly for the tourists' benefit, even on sunny days) this architectural spectacle turns into a concert. The water creates music. It gurgles through the drain pipes, spills over the cascades, roars in the funnels, rushes through the trumpet, trickles softly from the holes in the funnel down below, and streams out in a heavy jet at the end.

On sunny mornings, the metal plates which cover the facade of the sun house to the west, performs a silent but graceful play of light and shadow.

In St. Petersburg, wo sie in einer gemeinsamen WG lebten, ließen sich die Plastikerin Annette Paul und die Holzgestalter Christoph Roßner und André Tempel von der bizarren Architektur der Fallrohre faszinieren. Diese sind dort weit größer im Durchmesser als in Deutschland, laufen offen und in wilden Windungen über die Fassaden und befinden sich häufig in so schlechtem Zustand, daß sie bei heftigem Regen oder Frost ein Eigenleben zu führen beginnen. Oft genug stürzen sie dann auf und über die Straßen. Dieses Spektakel inspirierte die drei zu der Idee, ein solches Regentheater künstlerisch zu inszenieren. In St. Petersburg mußte das Projekt dann allerdings wegen Geldmangels aufgegeben werden.

Zurück in Dresden war Annette Paul eigentlich auf der Suche nach einer neuen Wohnung, weil es in ihre hineinregnete, als sie vom Wettbewerb zur Gestaltung der Kunsthöfe erfuhr. Natürlich erinnerte sie sich des alten Plans und begann mit den in ihrer Wohnung notgedrungen aufgestellten Wasserschüsseln, mit Trichtern und anderen Küchenutensilien schon mal versuchsweise einen »Geräuschbrunnen« zu bauen. Und André Tempel, der gerade am Chiemsee im Urlaub war, muß dort so lange bei Regen ins Wasser geschaut haben, daß er mit fast der gleichen Idee zurückkam.

As roommates in St. Petersburg, sculptor Annette Paul and designers Christoph Roßner and André Tempel were fascinated by the bizarre architecture of the drain pipes. The pipes there were much larger than those found in Germany, and due to their poor condition, tended to end their own lives by falling upon the streets whenever it rained or began to freeze. The three artists confess that this elemental spectacle served as the inspiration behind their idea for a »rain theatre.« However, due to lack of funding, these plans were not carried out immediately.
Back in Dresden, Annette Paul heard about the design contest for the Kunsthof Passage just as she was beginning the hunt for a new apartment. The leaky roof of her current place of residence suddenly reminded her of the plans for a rain theatre that she and her former roommates in St. Petersburg were never able to realize. Aided by the water that dripped serendipitously from the ceiling of her apartment, she started to experiment with making sounds by arranging bowls and other kitchen supplies to catch and channel the falling water. In the meantime, André Tempel, who had been spending some time at Lake Chiemsee, probably saw too much rain and water there, because he came back to Dresden with nearly the same idea.

55

DIE KÜNSTLER
The Artists

Ein Plan ist das eine, seine Durchführung bekanntlich das andere. Manche Idee mußte als undurchführbar verworfen werden. So war ursprünglich daran gedacht, das »Sonnenhaus« optisch ›schweben‹ zu lassen, indem man es mit einem breiten Sockel aus Spiegelfliesen versieht. Der ›Realismus‹ gebot leider, mit Verschmutzungen und Beschädigungen zu rechnen. Die zweite Version, die Spiegelfliesen auf der Fassade zu verteilen, hätte vielleicht die Nachbarn belästigen können und war überdies den Brandschutzverantwortlichen verdächtig. Und auch die Fallrohre am »Wasserhaus« erhielten erst am Bau – unter den fachkundigen Händen der ausführenden Handwerker und den kritischen Blicken der Künstler – ihre endgültige Form.

Als eigentliche Herausforderung erwies es sich jedoch, zu dritt gleichberechtigt an einem gemeinsamen Werk zu arbeiten. Drei Künstler – neun Meinungen. »Eine harte Probe für die Freundschaft«, erinnern sie sich mehr oder weniger gern. Zumindest dem Werk haben die angeblich heftigen Diskussionen letztlich offenbar nicht geschadet.

Having an idea and realizing it are two different things.
Many of the initial ideas had to be discarded for pragmatic reasons. One such idea was to let the sun house »hover« on a socket of mirror plates, but this model ultimately would have resulted in pollution and even damage to the plates.
The second version, which involved spreading the mirror plates over the surface of the facade, was also abandoned, as the sun reflecting into the neighbors' apartments would have most likely proved bothersome and, according to local firefighters, may have even created a fire hazard. In addition, the drain pipes did not find their final form until they had been fixed.
The most difficult challenge, however, was establishing an equal plane on which the three artists could express their individual ideas. Three artists equal three different opinions. Today they recall this time as a one which »really tested their friendship.« At least the alleged heated arguments did not harm the work itself.

Annette Paul
1970 in Görlitz als Annette Knothe geboren, studierte von 1991 bis 1992 an der Hochschule für Bildende Künste Dresden Restaurierung, wechselte dann zum Studium der Bildhauerei, das sie seither nur für zwei Babyjahre unterbrochen hat.

Christoph Roßner
1961 in Schlema geboren, lernte von 1978 bis 1981 Holzbildhauer und studierte von 1992 bis 1995 Design an der Fachhochschule für Angewandte Kunst in Schneeberg, lebt seitdem als freischaffender Künstler und Gestalter in Dresden

André Tempel
1970 in Schwedt (Oder) geboren, lernte 1986 bis 1988 Maschinen- und Anlagenmonteur, von 1992 bis 1996 studierte er Bildhauerei an der Fachhochschule für Angewandte Kunst in Schneeberg, lebt in Dresden

Annette Paul
was born Annette Knothe in 1970 in Görlitz, Saxony. After studying restoration at the Academy of Fine Arts (HfBK) in Dresden from 1991 to 1992, she shifted her focus to the study of sculpture. Since then, she has interrupted her studies twice to go on maternity leave.

Christoph Roßner
was born in 1961 in Schlema, Saxony. Rossner worked as an apprentice to a wood carver from 1978 to 1981. He later studied design at the School of Applied Art in Schneeberg, Saxony, from 1992 to 1995. Since then, he has lived in Dresden as a freelance artist and designer.

André Tempel
was born in 1970 in Schwedt/Oder. Following an apprenticeship as a machine fitter, he went on to study sculpture at the School of Applied Art in Schneeberg, Saxony, from 1992 to 1996, and now lives in Dresden.

57

WASSER IN DER KUNSTHOFPASSAGE
Water in the Kunsthof Passage

Schlangengleich zieht ein Wasserlauf durch den Hof der Fabelwesen. Im Hof des Lichts steht Schilf in einem künstlichen Sumpf. Im Hof der Metamorphosen rinnt leise, aber beharrlich ein kleiner Sandsteinbrunnen.
Und an der Fassade des Wasserhauses im Hof der Elemente finden halbstündlich die großen Wasserspiele statt (siehe S. 53). Wasser verbessert insbesondere an heißen Sommertagen das Mikroklima, das haben Gartengestalter zu allen Zeiten gewußt. Vor allem aber spülen ein paar Minuten »Wasser gucken« und »hören« den Großstadtstreß aus der Seele.

Trinkwasser kommt nicht aus der Wand, wie Städter, von denen jede(r) täglich 3 Liter davon trinkt und etwa 37 weitere zu anderen Zwecken verbraucht, zu glauben scheinen. Sauberes Grundwasser ist knapp und eigentlich zu kostbar für Wasserspiele, Brunnen oder die Toilettenspülung. Mit vergleichsweise geringem Aufwand wird deshalb in der Kunsthofpassage Regenwasser von den Dächern in Zisternen geleitet und als Brauchwasser verwendet. Auch das Oberflächenwasser der Höfe wird in den Brauchwasserkreislauf eingespeist.

Snakelike, water makes its way through the Courtyard of the Fabulous Creatures, while in the Courtyard of Light, reeds grow in an artificial swamp. In the Courtyard of the Metamorphoses, water spurts forth softly but persistently from a small sandstone fountain, and, in the Courtyard of the Elements, grand water festivals are staged every half an hour upon the facade of the water house. Just as landscape architects have always known, water has the ability to improve the microclimate substantially on hot summer days. Furthermore, a few minutes of looking and listening to water rinses big-city stress from the soul.

Drinking water does not magically flow from some inexhaustible source deep within the walls, as some city dwellers who drink approximately 3 liters and use an additional 37 for other purposes daily seem inclined to believe. Clean groundwater is limited, and the purification of surface water, expensive. Thus, the use of water in fountains, or even in toilet flushing systems, seems a blatant misuse of such a precious resource. Yet this is not the case in the Kunsthof Passage, where, with relatively small expenditure, rainwater is collected in cisterns to be used for such purposes.

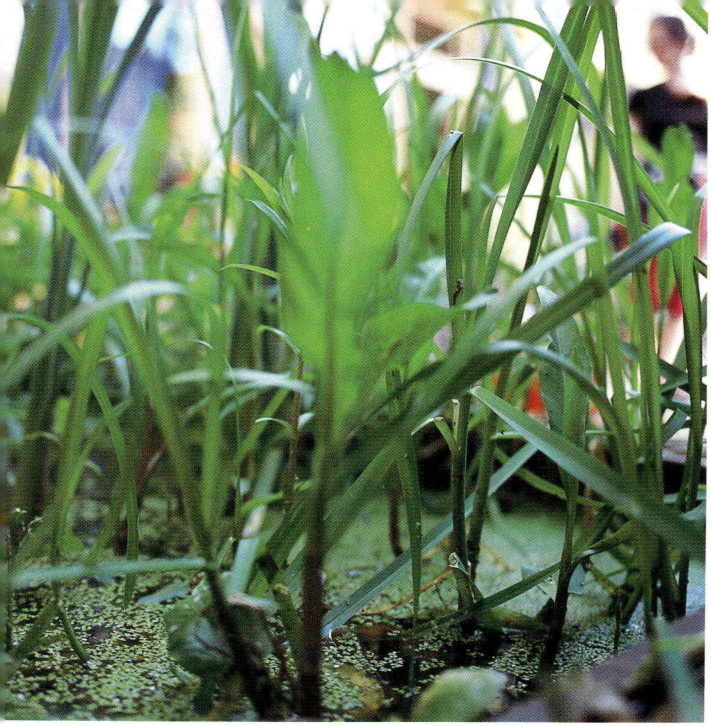

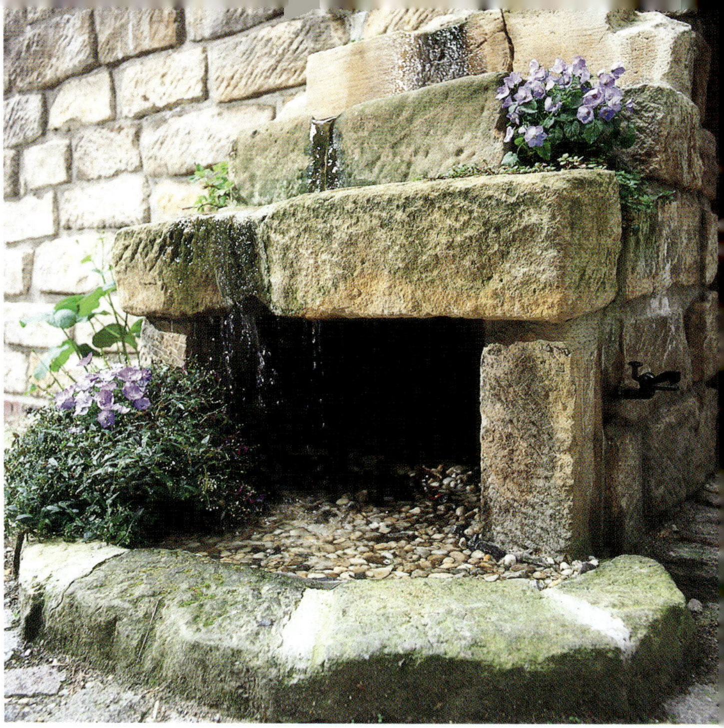

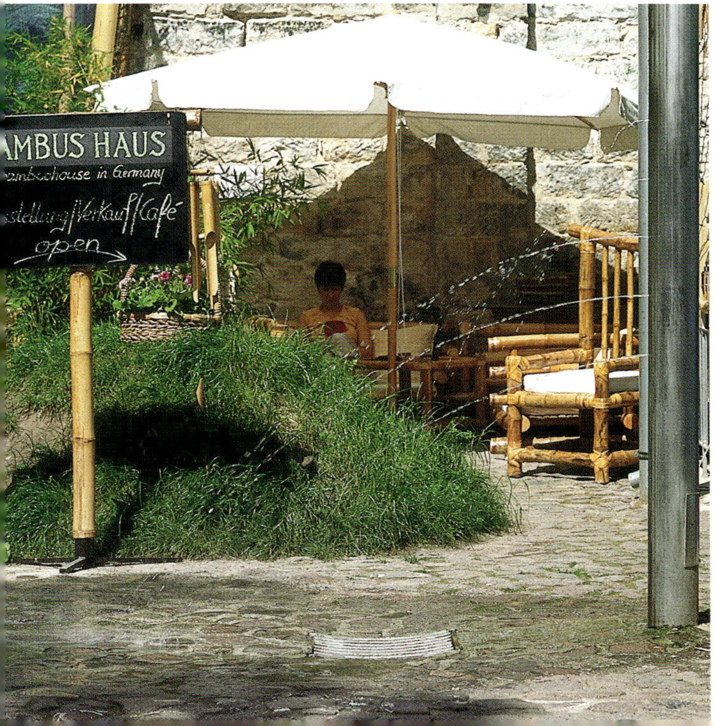
AMBUS HAUS
in Germany
Verkauf/Café
open

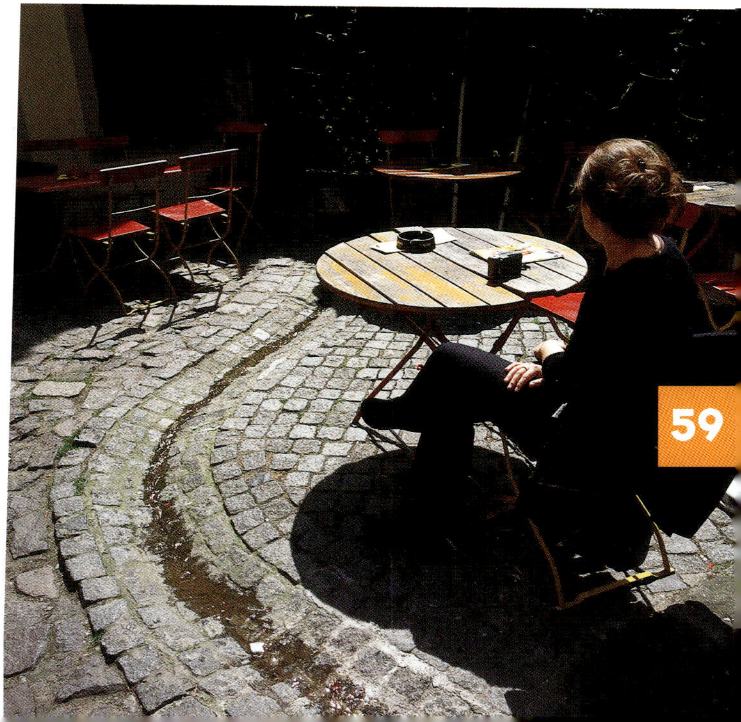

DANKSAGUNG
Acknowledgements

Für die finanzielle Unterstützung dieser Publikation danken wir:
Special thanks for financial support of this book:

Klaus Baumgart, Bad Mergentheim
Familie Lenz, Stuttgart und Dresden
Barbara Spielmann, München
Fa. Bau Schulze Projektsteuerung GmbH, Dresden
Fa. Maler Quaas GmbH & Co. KG, Meißen
Fa. OberländerSchneider GmbH, Freital
Fa. Opitz & Werner Bedachungen GmbH, Dresden
Fa. Tischlerei Markus Kaiser, Fischbach

Kunsthofpassage
Projektentwicklung
Project development:

GINKGO
← Projektentwicklung →

Hechtstraße 23, 01097 Dresden

Architekten / *Architects:*
Görlitzer Straße 25: Heike Böttcher
Görlitzer Straße 23: Knerer & Lang
Alaunstraße 70: Müller + Müller, Rivas + Zizelsberger

Besonderer Dank gilt den Bau-Handwerkern und -Handwerkerinnen der ausführenden Betriebe.

61

62

IMPRESSUM
Imprint

Die Deutsche Bibliothek – CIP-Einheitsaufnahme

Kunsthofpassage Dresden / Tankred Lenz; Eckhard Richter. [Holger Stein u.a. (Fotogr.)]. - Dresden: Thelem bei w.e.b., 2001
ISBN 3-935712-30-8

Dieses Buch ist für meine Eltern.
Tankred Lenz (Idee und Konzeption / idea and concept)

Dieses Buch ist für Marie Hering.
Herzlichen Dank an Walter Benjamin, dessen 1983 von Rolf Tiedemann unter dem Titel »Das Passagenwerk« bei Suhrkamp herausgegebene Materialsammlung ich als Steinbruch benutzt habe, den Kunsthofkünstlern für freundlich gewährte Interviews sowie Harald Kretzschmar und Grit Moch für Anregungen. Das Zitat von Peter Härtling (S. 4) stammt aus dessen Dresdner Poetikvorlesungen, die im Herbst 2001 unter dem Titel »Erinnerte Wirklichkeit – Erzählte Wahrheit« bei Thelem erscheinen, das anonyme Zitat auf S. 6 aus einem illustrierten Reiseführer von Paris, und ist dem »Passagenwerk« entnommen.
Eckhard Richter (Konzeption und Text / concept and text)

Dieses Buch ist für Marie-Luise und Jonathan.
Kathrin Augustin (Gestaltung und Layout / layout)

Dieses Buch ist für Daphne Mezereun.
Holger Stein (Fotografie / photographs)

I dedicate the book to Dr. John Martell, Jr., for his editorial assistance with this book and for all the other help he has given me over the years.
Tanya Pulver, Kalamazoo, MI (English texts)

© 2001 w.e.b. Universitätsverlag und Buchhandel
Bergstraße 78 ı D-01069 Dresden
Tel.: +49 (0351) 47 21 46 3 ı Fax: +49 (0351) 47 21 46 5
www.thelem.de
Thelem ist ein Imprint von w.e.b.
Alle Rechte vorbehalten. All rights reserved.
Herstellung: Druckerei Thieme, Meißen
Made in Germany.

Bildnachweis / *Pictures*

Holger Stein Fotografie, Dresden / *Holger Stein Photography, Dresden*	Seite / *Page* 2, 5, 10, 11, 13, 17, 18, 19, 21, 23, 25, 27, 30, 33, 41, 43, 44, 46, 51, 52, 55, 57, 59, 60, 62, 64, 65
Maximilian Britzger	22, 27
Tankred Lenz	9, 10, 11, 15, 17, 22, 27, 29, 34, 35, 37, 47, 49, 61, 62, 64, 65
Kirsten Mann	7, 60, 61
Viola Schöpe	22, 27, 28
Dana Westerlund	2. US, 17
Elke Wiedemann	11, 17, 41, 49
Jörg und Silva Wilking	7, 17
Torsten	17
Kathrin Stein	17
Imke Jörns	39
Harald Wandtke	3. US
SLUB/Dt. Fotothek/ Walter Möbius, 1934	13
Wochnik, 1986	14

www.kunsthofpassage.de

Alaunstraße 70

HOF DER FABELWESEN

Kunsthofpassage Dresden
Alaunstraße 70 / Görlitzer Str. 23 und 25, 01099 Dresden

Straßenbahn und Bus / *Public Transportation:*
Linie / No. 13 ➔ Alaunplatz / Bischofsweg
Linie / No. 3, 6, 7, 8, 11 ➔ Albertplatz oder Königsbrücker Straße

Eisenbahn, S-Bahn / *Railway, S-Bahn (Metropolitan Train)*
➔ Dresden Neustadt